S.O.A.R. WITH GOD

Daily Encouragement for Job Seekers

A 30-Day Devotional for Trusting God While You Search, Wait, and Prepare

Andrea C. McLean

ISBN: 978-1-963560-37-4

Printed in the United States of America

Dedication

Dedicated to every job seeker walking by faith in an uncertain season. May these pages remind you that God sees you, strengthens you, and guides each step ahead.

Table of Contents

A Sacred Season of Trust

The job search journey can be deeply personal. It is not only about finding work. It is also about navigating uncertainty, disappointment, and the challenge of trusting God when the path ahead is not fully clear.

Some days may feel hopeful. Other days may feel heavy. Questions about timing, provision, direction, and what comes next can rise quickly in a season like this.

Yet even here, this is still a sacred season.

S.O.A.R. with GOD was created to walk with you through this time with daily encouragement rooted in Scripture and reflection. Built around The S.O.A.R. Method®, this devotional will help you shift your mindset, overcome challenges, activate your plan, and reflect and refine as God leads you forward.

You may still be in transition, but you are not alone. God is with you in this sacred season of trust, and He will continue to guide each step ahead.

With grace,
Andrea

How to Use This Devotional

This devotional is designed for job seekers navigating transition, uncertainty, and preparation. You may be recovering from job loss, pursuing a new opportunity, changing direction, or re-entering the workforce.
You do not need extra time or a perfect routine. You need presence, honesty, and consistency.
Each day follows a simple rhythm.

Scripture

Each day begins with a Scripture reference drawn from the New International Version (NIV), followed by a short paraphrase so you can engage with the message wherever you are.

Reflection

The reflection connects Scripture to the emotional and practical realities of the job search journey. Read slowly and notice what encourages, challenges, or steadies you.

Journal Prompt

The journal prompt invites you to pause and respond honestly. There is no right answer. Write what is true for you today.

The S.O.A.R. Framework

This devotional is structured around The S.O.A.R. Method®, a simple framework designed to help you stay grounded in faith while navigating the job search journey.

Shift Your Mindset

Days 1–7 focus on renewing your thinking and anchoring your identity in God.

Overcome Challenges

Days 8–15 address rejection, discouragement, and uncertainty with faith and steadiness.

Activate Your Plan

Days 16–23 focus on faithful action, wise preparation, courage, and practical next steps.

Reflect and Refine

Days 24–30 help you notice what God is teaching you and carry it forward with trust.

How to approach each day

Read one day at a time.
Choose a consistent time if possible.
Write honestly, not perfectly.
Return to earlier pages when needed.

Shift Your Mindset

Renew your thinking and anchor your identity in God as you begin this season.

God Sees You in This Season

Scripture

Psalm 33:18

God watches over those who place their hope in Him.

Reflection

A job search can make you feel overlooked. Applications go out, responses are delayed, and silence can start to feel personal. But God has not lost sight of you. He sees your effort, your questions, and the weight you carry each day. Your worth is not reduced by waiting or by a closed door. Even in this uncertain season, you are fully seen, fully known, and still held in God's care.

Journal Prompt

Where have I been feeling unseen or overlooked in this season, and what would change if I truly believed God sees me fully?

Journal Reflections

Your Identity is Bigger Than Your Job Title

Scripture
Ephesians 2:10

You were created by God with purpose, and your life still holds meaningful work.

Reflection
When work feels uncertain, it is easy to let your title shape your sense of worth. But your identity was never meant to rest on a role alone. You are not defined by a company, a position, or a paycheck. God created you with purpose long before this season began. A job may change, but your value does not. Begin here, rooted in who God says you are, not in what your current circumstances suggest.

Journal Prompt
What parts of my identity have I tied too closely to work, and what truth do I need to remember about who I am in God?

Journal Reflections

Choose Faith Over Panic

Scripture

Philippians 4:6

Bring every worry to God instead of carrying it alone.

Reflection

A job search can create urgency, but urgency and panic are not the same. Panic clouds your thinking and pulls your focus toward fear. Faith steadies you. It reminds you that God is still present, even when the outcome is not clear. You do not have to force the future into place. You can bring your concerns to God, take the next wise step, and trust Him to guide what you cannot control.

Journal Prompt

Where has panic been shaping my thoughts or decisions, and what would it look like to respond in faith instead?

Journal Reflections

Releasing the Need to Control the Outcome

Scripture

Proverbs 3:5

Trust God fully, even when the path ahead does not make sense to you.

Reflection

Uncertainty often awakens the need to control every detail. You want to know when the answer will come, how it will unfold, and what to do next. But peace does not come from controlling the outcome. It comes from trusting God with what is beyond your reach. You are called to be faithful in what you can do. God will guide the rest. Let go of what you were never meant to carry alone.

Journal Prompt

What outcome, timeline, or expectation am I trying to control, and what would it mean to surrender it to God today?

Journal Reflections

Trusting God in the Waiting

Scripture

Isaiah 40:31

As you wait on God, He renews your strength and carries you forward.

Reflection

Waiting can feel like nothing is happening. But waiting is not the same as being forgotten. God is still at work in the silence, in the delay, and in the parts of the journey you cannot yet see. He is strengthening your heart and preparing what is ahead in ways that may not be visible yet. This season may be slower than you want, but it is not empty. Trust can deepen here if you let it.

Journal Prompt

What is this season of waiting revealing about my trust in God, and how can I stay anchored while I wait?

Journal Reflections

You Are Still Called

Scripture

Romans 11:29

What God has placed in you remains steady and cannot be taken away.

Reflection

A difficult season can make you question your direction and doubt your gifts. But transition does not cancel your calling. A delay does not erase what God placed in you. You are still gifted, still needed, and still capable of meaningful impact. What feels uncertain right now has not changed God's purpose for your life. Do not let disappointment shrink your vision. You are still called, even here.

Journal Prompt

Where have I started to doubt my calling, and what do I need to remember about the gifts and purpose God has placed in me?

Journal Reflections

Preparing Your Heart for the Journey

Scripture
Proverbs 4:23

Protect your heart carefully, because it shapes the course of your life.

Reflection
A job search is not only about opportunities. It also affects your heart. What settles in you during this season will shape how you think, respond, and move forward. Guarding your heart matters. Fear, bitterness, and comparison can quietly take root if left unchecked. But when your heart stays anchored in God, you can move with greater steadiness. Ask Him to strengthen you from the inside as you continue this journey.

Journal Prompt
What condition is my heart in right now, and what do I need God to strengthen, heal, or steady in me as I continue this journey?

Journal Reflections

Overcome Challenges

*Face rejection, discouragement, and
uncertainty with faith and steadiness.*

When Rejection Feels Personal

Scripture
Jeremiah 31:3

God's love for you is lasting, steady, and unchanged.

Reflection
Rejection can stir deeper questions about worth, value, and whether you are enough. But rejection is an event, not an identity. It may reflect timing, fit, or factors you cannot see. It does not define your future, and it does not change how God sees you. You do not have to deny the sting of disappointment. Just do not build your identity around it. You are still loved, still capable, and still moving forward.

Journal Prompt
What rejection have I been carrying personally, and what truth do I need to speak over myself today?

Journal Reflections

Fighting Discouragement

Scripture
Galatians 6:9

Do not give up, because your faithfulness will bear fruit in time.

Reflection
Discouragement often builds quietly. One delay leads to another, and over time your energy begins to fade. It can make you wonder whether your effort matters at all. But discouragement does not get to decide your next step. Feeling tired does not mean you are failing. It means you need renewal. God sees your persistence, and He can strengthen you again. Take the next faithful step, even if it is smaller than yesterday's.

Journal Prompt
Where has discouragement been draining my energy, and what is one faithful step I can still take today?

Journal Reflections

DAY 10
When Doors Stay Closed

Scripture
Revelation 3:7

The doors God opens cannot be blocked, and those He closes cannot be reopened by human effort.

Reflection
Closed doors can feel confusing and painful, especially when you have prepared well and hoped deeply. But not every closed door is a punishment. Some are protection. Some are redirection. God sees what you cannot. He knows which opportunities are right for you and which ones are not. What feels disappointing now may later reveal itself as mercy. Trust that what God allows to stay closed is not beyond His wisdom or care.

Journal Prompt
What closed door have I been struggling to accept, and how might God be using it to protect or redirect me?

Journal Reflections

Resisting Comparison

Scripture

Galatians 6:5

Stay focused on what is yours to carry and walk faithfully in your own path.

Reflection

Comparison can quietly drain your peace during a job search. Someone else's progress can start to feel like proof that you are behind. But God is not writing your story by copying someone else's. Your path, your timing, and your preparation are your own. Another person's breakthrough does not take away from what God is doing in you. Stay focused on your journey. Peace grows when you stop measuring your life against someone else's timeline.

Journal Prompt

Where has comparison been affecting my peace, and what would it look like to focus fully on my own path?

Journal Reflections

DAY 12
Staying Steady in Uncertainty

Scripture
Psalm 46:1

God is your safe place and your strength when life feels uncertain.

Reflection
Uncertainty can make everything feel unsettled. When you do not know what is coming next, it is easy to feel unsteady in your thoughts and emotions. But uncertainty does not mean God is uncertain. He already sees what you cannot see. Your peace does not have to depend on having all the answers. It can rest in the One who holds them. Ask God to steady you, even while the details are still unfolding.

Journal Prompt
What uncertainty has been affecting me most, and how can I anchor myself in God instead of in answers?

Journal Reflections

God Is Working While You Wait

Scripture
Exodus 14:14

Rest in God's care and trust that He is working for you.

Reflection
When nothing seems to be moving, it is easy to assume nothing is happening. But God works in places you cannot always see. He works in timing, in preparation, in relationships, and in the quiet shaping of your heart. The absence of visible progress does not mean He is absent. Waiting may feel slow, but it is not wasted. Trust that God is active in the unseen, even when the path ahead is still hidden.

Journal Prompt
Where have I assumed nothing is happening, and how would my perspective shift if I trusted that God is working in the unseen?

Journal Reflections

Strength for Another Day

Scripture

2 Corinthians 12:9

When you feel weak, God will sustain you with His grace and strength.

Reflection

Some days feel heavier than others. The effort of trying again can feel like more than you have the strength to carry. But weakness is not failure. It is often where you become most aware of your need for God's grace. He does not ask you to be strong on your own. He meets you in your limits and gives strength for today. Not for the whole journey, just for the next step in front of you.

Journal Prompt

Where do I feel weak right now, and what would it look like to receive God's grace for just this day?

Journal Reflections

Hope That Does Not Collapse

Scripture

Romans 15:13

As you trust God, He strengthens your heart with hope and peace.

Reflection

After enough disappointment, hope can begin to feel risky. You may want to protect yourself by expecting less. But biblical hope is not rooted in ideal circumstances. It is rooted in the character of God. That means it can remain steady even when life feels uncertain. Let your hope rest in who God is, not in one opportunity or timeline. When hope is anchored in Him, it can bend under pressure without breaking.

Journal Prompt

What has my hope been resting on, and how can I root it more deeply in God's faithfulness?

Journal Reflections

Activate Your Plan

Take faithful, practical steps as you search, prepare, and move forward.

Faith Requires Movement

Scripture
James 2:17

Faith comes alive when it is lived out through action.

Reflection

Trusting God does not mean becoming passive. Faith moves. It prays, listens, and then takes the next wise step. Waiting on God is not the same as doing nothing. Often, He gives direction as you move with intention and trust. A job search requires action, even when emotions feel unsteady. Update the résumé. Send the message. Submit the application. Let your faith be active, not frozen. God can guide you as you go.

Journal Prompt

What action have I been delaying, and what would it look like to take that step in faith today?

Journal Reflections

Showing Up with Excellence

Scripture
Colossians 3:23

Whatever you do, give your best effort as an offering to God.

Reflection

When the process feels long, it can be tempting to rush, settle, or stop giving your best. But excellence still matters. It is not about perfection. It is about care, intention, and stewardship. The way you prepare, communicate, and follow through reflects your character. Even in a difficult season, you can still show up with diligence and integrity. You may not control the outcome, but you can control how you carry yourself through the process.

Journal Prompt
Where can I bring more excellence to my job search, and what specific area needs more attention from me right now?

Journal Reflections

Courage to Reach Out

Scripture

Joshua 1:9

Do not give in to fear. God is with you wherever you go.

Reflection

Reaching out takes courage. It can feel vulnerable to ask for a conversation, make a connection, or let others know you are searching. Fear may tell you to stay quiet and avoid the risk of being ignored. But God often works through people, relationships, and conversations. One message can open a door, bring clarity, or offer encouragement. Do not let discomfort keep you isolated. Take the step. Courage often begins before confidence does.

Journal Prompt

Who do I need to reach out to, and what fear do I need to move past in order to do it?

Journal Reflections

Stewarding What Is in Your Hands

Scripture
Luke 16:10

Faithfulness in small things matters deeply to God.

Reflection

It is easy to focus on what is missing. But stewardship begins with what is already in your hands. You still have experience, skills, insight, time, and the ability to prepare well. You still have choices you can make today that will shape tomorrow. God does not ask you to manage what you do not have. He asks you to be faithful with what you do. Your next step may begin with honoring what is already present.

Journal Prompt

What has God already placed in my hands in this season, and how can I steward it more faithfully?

Journal Reflections

Preparing for the Right Opportunity

Scripture
Proverbs 24:27

Put in the preparation now so you are ready for what comes next.

Reflection
Preparation is an act of faith. It says you believe God can open the right door, and you want to be ready when He does. Preparation is not only about applying for roles. It is also about clarifying your direction, refining your message, strengthening your materials, and growing your confidence. When you prepare well, you reduce panic and increase readiness. Do not just hope for the next opportunity. Get ready for it with intention.

Journal Prompt
What do I need to prepare now so I am ready when the right opportunity comes?

Journal Reflections

Wisdom for Your Next Step

Scripture
James 1:5

When you need direction, ask God, and He will guide you in wisdom.

Reflection

Not every next step is obvious. You may be weighing options, considering a pivot, or wondering when to move. In moments like this, information helps, but wisdom matters more. Wisdom helps you discern what is right, not just what is available. God invites you to ask for that kind of guidance. He is not withholding clarity from you. Bring your decisions before Him and trust that He can lead you one step at a time.

Journal Prompt

What decision or next step do I need wisdom for right now, and have I truly invited God into that process?

Journal Reflections

Let Your Words Reflect Confidence

Scripture
Colossians 4:6

Let your words reflect grace and truth.

Reflection
The way you speak about yourself matters. Your words shape how others hear your value, but they also reflect what you believe about yourself. A difficult season can make your language hesitant or uncertain. But confidence does not mean exaggerating. It means speaking truthfully about your experience, strengths, and contribution. Let your words reflect clarity, not fear. Tell your story with honesty, grace, and the quiet confidence that comes from knowing your worth.

Journal Prompt
How have I been speaking about myself in this season, and where do I need to let my words reflect more truth and confidence?

Journal Reflections

Trust God, Then Take the Step

Scripture
Proverbs 3:6

Invite God into every step, and He will show you where to go.

Reflection
There comes a point when you must stop circling and move forward. You may not feel fully ready, and you may not have every answer. But after you have prayed, prepared, and sought wisdom, faith often looks like taking the step in front of you. Trust grows in motion. Confidence often comes after obedience, not before it. Do not wait for perfect certainty. Trust God, then take the next step with the peace He provides.

Journal Prompt
What step is in front of me right now, and what would it look like to trust God enough to take it?

Journal Reflections

Reflect and Refine

Notice what God is teaching you and carry it forward with trust.

Pause and Notice What God Has Taught You

Scripture
Psalm 105:5

Remember what God has done and do not forget His faithfulness.

Reflection
When you are focused on what still has not happened, it is easy to miss what God has already been teaching you. But every season leaves lessons. This one may have revealed where you needed deeper trust, greater patience, or a stronger sense of identity. Reflection helps you see that this journey has not been empty. Even if it has been hard, it has not been wasted. Pause long enough to notice what God has been shaping in you.

Journal Prompt
What has God been teaching me in this season that I do not want to miss?

Journal Reflections

Refining Your Direction

Scripture
Isaiah 30:21

God will guide you and show you where to walk.

Reflection
Sometimes a job search does more than open new options. It also clarifies what matters most to you now. What once felt right may no longer fit. What you once pursued may no longer align with the person you are becoming. This is not confusion. It is refinement. God can use this season to sharpen your discernment and help you recognize what belongs in your next chapter. Pay attention to what has become clearer as you move forward.

Journal Prompt
How has this season been refining what I want, need, or value in my next opportunity?

Journal Reflections

DAY 26

Closed Doors Can Redirect You

Scripture

Proverbs 16:9

You may make your plans, but God is the one who guides your steps.

Reflection

Some closed doors make more sense with time. What felt painful at first may later reveal itself as redirection. God can use what did not happen to guide you toward what should. He can move you away from what would have drained you and toward what better fits your calling and season. Redirection does not always feel gentle in the moment, but it can still be grace. Ask God to help you see closed doors through that lens.

Journal Prompt

What closed door might I need to view through the lens of redirection instead of defeat?

Journal Reflections

Gratitude in the Middle of the Search

Scripture

1 Thessalonians 5:18

Choose gratitude in every season.

Reflection

Gratitude can feel difficult when your answer has not arrived yet. But gratitude is not only for the end of the journey. It has power in the middle of it too. It helps you notice what is still good, still true, and still present, even in an unfinished season. It reminds you that God's faithfulness is not on hold. Name what you can thank Him for today. Gratitude can steady your spirit while you wait.

Journal Prompt

What can I thank God for today, even in the middle of this unfinished season?

Journal Reflections

Trusting God's Timing

Scripture
Ecclesiastes 3:11

God brings things together beautifully in His time.

Reflection
Timing can be one of the hardest parts of a job search. You may feel ready, willing, and eager to move, yet the answer still does not come when you expect it. But delay is not always denial. Sometimes timing is part of the preparation. God's timing may not match your preference, but it is never careless. Keep preparing, keep praying, and keep trusting. What feels slow to you is still fully visible to Him.

Journal Prompt
Where have I been struggling with God's timing, and what would it look like to trust Him more deeply in that area?

Journal Reflections

Becoming Stronger in the Journey

Scripture
Romans 5:3–4

Hard seasons can grow perseverance, character, and lasting hope within you.

Reflection
This season may not be the one you would have chosen, but it may be strengthening you in important ways. Hard seasons build endurance, deepen faith, and shape character. You may already be stronger than you realize. Not because everything feels easier, but because you have kept going. You have continued to show up, learn, adapt, and trust. That kind of strength will serve you long after this season ends. God is forming something solid in you.

Journal Prompt
In what ways have I grown stronger through this journey, even if the process has been difficult?

Journal Reflections

Moving Forward with Faith

Scripture

2 Corinthians 5:7

Keep walking forward by faith, even when you cannot yet see the full picture.

Reflection

As this devotional comes to a close, your journey may still be unfolding. But you are not leaving empty-handed. You are carrying truth, growth, and a deeper awareness of God's presence. Faith does not require full visibility. It trusts God enough to keep moving. So keep praying, keep preparing, and keep taking the next wise step. What comes next may still be forming, but you do not walk into it alone. God will continue to guide you.

Journal Prompt

As I move forward from here, what does it look like for me to continue this journey with faith?

Journal Reflections

Closing Reflection

As you reach the end of this devotional, take a moment to notice what has shifted in you. The journey may still be unfolding, but you have made space to reflect, pray, and move forward with greater intention.

Through this season, God has been with you. He has seen your effort, your questions, your disappointment, and your hope. He has continued to strengthen you, guide you, and remind you that your worth is not defined by a title, a timeline, or an outcome. As you continue your journey, keep trusting, keep preparing, and keep taking the next wise step in faith.

About the Author

Andrea C. McLean is a board-certified life, career, and executive coach, author, and speaker who helps people navigate transition with clarity, confidence, and purpose.

After more than three decades in global corporate leadership, Andrea shifted her focus to coaching and writing, supporting individuals as they move through change, redefine success, and design what comes next. Her work centers on intentional growth, grounded leadership, and aligning daily decisions with long-term purpose.

Andrea is the founder of ACM Coaching Group and the creator of The S.O.A.R. Method®, a framework designed to help people shift their mindset, overcome challenges, activate their plan, and reflect with intention.

Also by Andrea C. McLean

For personal growth and encouragement:
Decide to Be Your Future Self
The F.L.A.P. Method®

For faith-centered support in transition:
S.O.A.R. with GOD for Women in Leadership Transition
S.O.A.R. with GOD for Men in Leadership Transition

For more encouragement, coaching, and resources,
visit: andreacmclean.com

www.ingramcontent.com/pod-product-compliance
Lightning Source LLC
Chambersburg PA
CBHW021341060726
47591CB00006B/2124